BRITISH RAILWAYS

PAST and PRESENT
Special

THE FFESTINIOG AND WELSH HIGHLAND
RAILWAYS

Welsh Highland and Festiniog Railways

Zig-zagging through Glorious Welsh Mountain and Lake Scenery

MAGNIFICENT VIEWS UNOBTAINABLE BY ANY OTHER MEANS
ENCHANTING AND UNRIVALLED SCENERY THROUGHOUT

In conjunction with the L. M. & S. Rly. one of the Best & Cheapest Day Tours in Great Britain can be made every week-day (except Saturdays) from July 20th to September 11th, 1931

FIVE VALLEYS CIRCULAR TOUR

Embracing the Valleys of Conway, Lledr, Maentwrog, Glaslyn and Gwyrfai
Beautiful Bettws-y-Coed, Blaenau Festiniog,
Picturesque Port Madoc, The Pass of Aberglaslyn,
The Alpine Village of Beddgelert,
South Snowdon, Quellyn Lake,
Caernarvon and its Castle,
Bangor with its Cathedral and Colleges.

SEE OTHER SIDE FOR A DESCRIPTIVE ROUTE OF THE TOUR

From	Times of starting via Festiniog	Third Class Inclusive Fare for the Tour
LLANDUDNO	10-25 a.m.	7/11
COLWYN BAY	10-29 a.m.	8/-
RHYL	10-15 a.m.	9/3

Children under 3 years of age free, between 3 and 14 years of age half-fares

The Tour can, also, be made in the reverse direction, (via Caernarvon)

From	Times of starting	
Llandudno	11-5 a.m.	
Colwyn Bay	11-4 a.m.	At the same Fares
Rhyl	10-44 a.m.	

Passengers must state at time of booking which way they elect to travel

SEE THE BEAUTIES OF WALES IN SAFETY AND COMFORT—WET OR FINE

Further particulars at the Stations or from Welsh Highland & Festiniog Railways, Portmadoc

SEE OVER

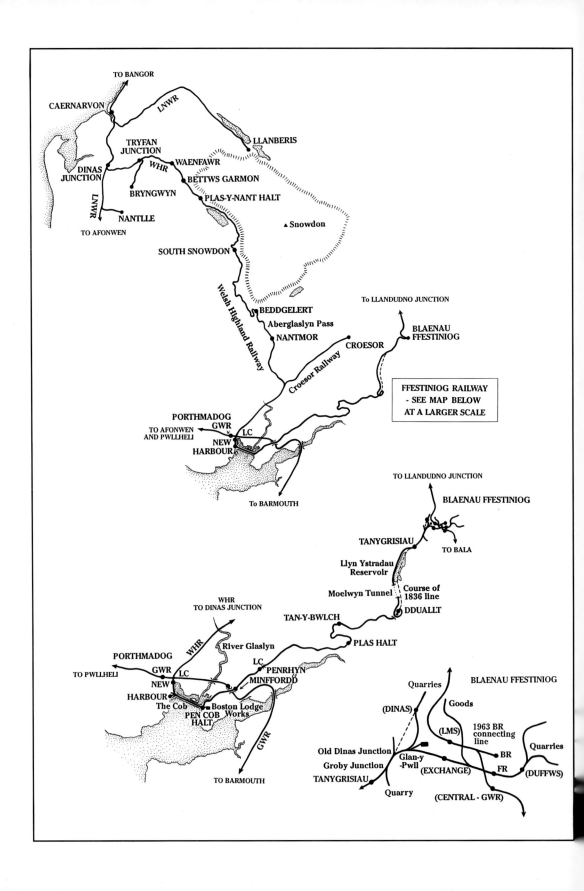

BRITISH RAILWAYS

PAST and PRESENT
Special

THE FFESTINIOG AND WELSH HIGHLAND
RAILWAYS

*A nostalgic trip along both lines from
Caernarvon to Porthmadog and
Blaenau Ffestiniog*

John Stretton

FESTINIOG RAILWAY.	FESTINIOG RAILWAY.
FREE TICKET.—FIRST CLASS.	FREE TICKET.—FIRST CLASS.
_____DEPARTMENT.	_____DEPARTMENT.
No. 9	No. 9 Train,_____187
Date	From____to____
Name	Name
Train____o'Clock,	Why granted____
From	
To	Head of Department.
Why granted	N.B.—Free Tickets are granted to persons employed on the Company's Business only, and must be given up when demanded.

Past and
Present

Past & Present Publishing Ltd

First published in March 1996

British Library Cataloguing in Publication Data

A catalogue record for this book is available from the British Library

ISBN 1 85895 091 0

Past & Present Publishing Ltd
Unit 5
Home Farm Close
Church Street
Wadenhoe
Peterborough PE8 5TE
Tel/fax (01832) 720440

Map on page 2 drawn by Christina Siviter; other maps by the author

Printed and bound in Great Britain

ACKNOWLEDGEMENTS

I have derived many hours of genuine pleasure in researching and photographing the two railways; I hope that you the reader can share some of this. I have been aided and abetted by people too numerous to mention in total, but I would particularly wish to thank Jim Slater, Hilary Davies, Adrian Gray, John Ewing, Francis Stapleton, John Keylock, Andrew Morris, Colin Dukes, Jon Marsh and Terry Gough. In addition, special thanks are due to Gordon Rushton and others on the FR for their help and support, and to Paul Davies, whose enthusiasm, knowledge, companionship, patience and excruciatingly bad jokes have been a real asset! Thanks are also due to my wife, Judi, for her support, and to my daughter Tammy, a volunteer on the FR and for whom the railway as a whole and *Merddin Emrys* in particular are heaven on earth!

ABBREVIATIONS

Various initials have been used in the text; for clarity, they stand for:

FR	Festiniog/Ffestiniog Railway
WHR	Welsh Highland Railway (both old and new)
NWNGR	North Wales Narrow Gauge Railways
PB&SSR	Portmadoc, Beddgelert & South Snowdon Railway Company
LNWR	London & North Western Railway
LMS	London, Midland & Scottish Railway
GWR	Great Western Railway

CONTENTS

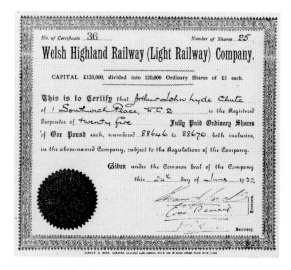

FOREWORD
by
Gordon Rushton
General Manager, Ffestiniog Railway, 1991-96

Looking at the Ffestiniog Railway today, the apparent effortless ease with which *David Lloyd George* hauls a train of ten well-filled bogie coaches up the steady grade, to the accompaniment of a melodious Gresley chime whistle, suggests that it has always been like this. Behind the scenes, the occasional struggle with locomotives and carriages being seemingly disobliging reminds those involved of the continuous battle between men and machines to get the performance we all take for granted. It is very difficult to remember that the railway is always evolving. Only when a colour-slide reveals that a fence here has gone, flat-bottomed rail has replaced bullhead, or flaky paint has been replaced with the shining variety, do we notice the contrast. It is good to look back and see where we came from. Especially now, when poised on the threshold of a new adventure, which when it matures will change the railway again.

In fact it has always been this way. What we think of as permanent is only a snapshot. The Ffestiniog started as a horse tramway; imagine the pace of change in the 1860s when it was re-engineered as a steam railway. Major changes were needed to keep pace with the rapid rise in slate traffic. The Ffestiniog was at the forefront of technology then, with articulated locomotive power and bogie carriages being advances worthy of note to the world at large. Even during the years of decline, from the 1920s to the outbreak of war in 1939, change was proceeding apace. Not palatable change perhaps - it culminated in closure - but change nevertheless.

In the 1950s revival brought massive upheaval. The nature of the railway changed, from slate carrier to tourist attraction. The new role set precedents never before seen: engines from other railways, corridor coaches on the narrow gauge, buffet cars, loos on the train, people giving their time free. The new enterprise prospered and expanded. The things that didn't change, like the scenery and the excellent engineering of the railway, were seen as major advantages.

Other changes resulted in major disappointment. The line near to Tanygrisiau was flooded to build a pumped-storage power station, and an entirely new section had to be built to rejoin with the old. In fact, today this change is understood to have brought fundamental benefits that were not seen then. The restrictive loading gauge of the old Moelwyn Tunnel was relaxed, new carriages were built with greater headroom and locomotives expanded to give the crews more space. The corridor cars promoted the foundation for customer-service-at-seat from the buffet car, and it is that feature that gives today's Ffestiniog the main-line feel. Even a very

Left **Exactly 100 years apart, to the minute! The glass negative of the top photograph, showing *Merddin Emrys* standing at Portmadoc, states that the photograph was taken at 12.30 pm on 19 September 1895. One hundred years later, the same engine is still in active service and the Ffestiniog Railway arranged for it to be in the same place at precisely 12.30 pm on 19 September 1995!**

The FR is probably unique in being able to carry out this trick, having the same engine in everyday service and standing on the same spot; and the views provide a fascinating mix of just how much has changed and how much is still extant. The engine has obviously received tender loving care, to enhance its present highly attractive maroon livery, and there are many detail differences, not least the transition from coal burning to being oil-fired, but it is undeniably the same engine, and even the connecting rods are in the same position! Behind, this area of Porthmadog has seen changes, with the Foundry gone, but Britannia Terrace is relatively little changed, apart from the houses now looking much smarter than a century ago! 1995 driver Peter Lawson does his best to emulate his forebear - the epitome of the joy of past and present comparisons. *Kirklees Leisure Services/MJS*

careful look at the photographs from the past does not quite reveal that today locomotives are adjusted or built to a scale of 13 inches to the foot! To see this one has to compare the gloriously restored *Palmerston* next to older brother *Prince*.

The new administration on the Ffestiniog really got the bit between its teeth. As a direct successor to the old company, the notion of a railway 'preserved' has been resisted. Sometimes things got a little out of hand, and perhaps the two examples of Double-Fairlies, *Earl of Merioneth* built in 1979 and *David Lloyd George* built in 1993, bear witness to changes in attitudes over the decades. If the Ffestiniog lost its way a little in the 1980s, it was because of the severe austerity imposed to survive the outpouring of expenditure in reopening to Blaenau Ffestiniog. By the 1990s the line was blooming; the era of Eurogrants had arrived and much new equipment was being built. This fillip to morale was heightened by brighter carriage liveries, and it was discovered that locomotives did not have to be green by order of Providence.

Better still, the railway no longer remained an exclusive male preserve and these influences began to make their appearance in lineside gardens, cleaner trains and the emergence of volunteering by whole families. This wasn't because of any division of duties; it arose because the newcomers noticed changes that needed to be made that the incumbents hadn't thought of importance. At the same time the policy of improvement of customer service developed, just in time to satisfy a tourist market that was rapidly increasing its expectations.

One interesting and delightful outcome of the gradual emergence of prosperity has been the achieved desire to preserve the large collection of original equipment in working order. In the early days of restoration the fact that the impoverished old company couldn't afford to throw things away was a godsend to the revivalists. As traffic grew, they pulled the old relics from the sidings where they had lain for years, overhauled them and set them to work. Today we are used to having locomotives from the 1860s and carriages from the 1870s in regular service. We have to be reminded by colleagues from the National Railway Museum that this makes the Ffestiniog Railway unique. In recent years ancient machines have been restored to period condition, and stations are being reinstated as they were in the last century. A delightful paradox arises from these activities as we may now recreate scenes *unchanged* from former eras, and at the same time gain pleasure from having diametrically opposed, shiny, modern trains.

The Ffestiniog has always been a little railway doing a big job. It carries more people than all but one of Britain's private railways, and the big boys are standard gauge! Goodness knows how successful it will be in the future, but one thing is certain, it will be different from the way it is now. Change has been with us in every decade. Look over the pages following and you will see this to be true.

INTRODUCTION

The months of March and October 1995 were very important for both the Ffestiniog and Welsh Highland Railways. On 14 March the Secretary of State for Transport made the Welsh Highland Railway Transfer Order, vesting in the Festiniog Railway Company the powers to take over from the Liquidator the rights to the old WHR route; then, in October, the FR was awarded £4.3m from the National Lottery Millennium Fund towards the cost of building the first section of the new WHR, from Caernarvon to Rhyd Ddu. Thus was the door nudged open to reveal a tantalising glimpse of the possibility of seeing trains once more running on this superb stretch of line by the end of the millennium.

This is not an extension of the FR, but a new railway to be run in conjunction and in harmony with its older neighbour, to the benefit of both, and certainly to the potentially enormous benefit of travellers to the area. And it is entirely appropriate that the FR and WHR should work hand in hand, as there was much similar intermingling some 70 years ago.

The Festiniog Railway was born in 1836, but its antecedents stretch back to the beginning of the century and the vision of William Maddocks MP. Owner of the Tanyrallt Estate and creator of the village of Tremadoc, on land reclaimed by him from the tidal salt marsh, his was a grandiose scheme to bridge Traeth Mawr by a huge mile-long stone embankment, slicing straight across the Glaslyn estuary and partitioning the inland valley from the sea. The first attempt, completed in 1811, was breached by a storm the following winter, and it was not until 1814 that Maddocks was finally successful in shutting out the sea. He then proceeded to build a harbour at the western end, and the town of Portmadoc was born - it did not exist in 1800! A horse tramway was built on the embankment, to connect with any trade from the east, but Maddocks was not to see the benefits of his endeavours, dying penniless in 1827.

The railway came into being from the need of Samuel Holland to move slate from his Rhiwbryfdir quarry at Blaenau Ffestiniog to the waiting ships at Portmadoc. This was to satisfy the mushrooming demand for slate from burgeoning English industrial towns. After a labour of seven years, and with the help of a number of well-met individuals with railway and/or engineering qualifications and experience, the line saw birth on 20 April 1836, being the first in the world to have tamed such wild terrain. Although sanctioned for steam engines, it initially used horses to haul the empties up the gradient and 'free' gravity to send the loaded wagons down to the port. With the exception of two rope-operated inclines to surmount an outcrop of Moelwyn Mountain, which lasted for the first eight years of the railway until a tunnel could be built, the line had cleverly been laid to provide a continuous falling gradient from Blaenau Ffestiniog - a very far-sighted concept!

Success was immediate and traffic rapidly grew, as did the towns of Portmadoc and Blaenau Ffestiniog. It was soon obvious that horses were inadequate and locomotives would be needed, but none existed at the time to run on such a narrow gauge as 1 ft 11½ in, and even the famed Robert Stephenson had declared the idea to be impossible. It was not, of course, and after various speculative designs had been considered and discarded, George England & Co of London delivered four 0-4-0STs - *Princess* (the first to be steamed), *Palmerston*, *Prince* and *Mountaineer* - in the summer of 1863.

Over the ensuing years traffic continued to grow, requiring more powerful locomotives, and, like the answer to a maiden's prayer, Robert Fairlie appeared on the scene at just the right time, in 1869. He had an 1863-dated patent for a 'double' locomotive and was anxious to prove his ideas. *Little Wonder* was commissioned from George England & Co in 1869 and from its first runs at the turn of 1870 it proved to be a great success, impressing a specially invited gathering of international railway magnates. Since that time the Festiniog Railway has been renowned for its use of these engines, and the Company's own Boston Lodge Works has built four of them, the latest, *David Lloyd George*, at the beginning of the current decade.

Inevitably, the line's prosperity attracted jealous eyes, and the London & North Western Railway (in 1879) and the Great Western Railway (1883) both made their way to Blaenau Ffestiniog. This obviously impacted on the FR's trade, and the heyday and splendid isolation of the railway was over. Traffic declined over the years, until by 1945 only 9,000 tons of slate was carried (compared to a peak of 139,000 in 1897!), and on 1 August 1946 the last train ran.

For the next eight years the railway had an air of 'Marie Celeste' about it, as it was left as if the last shift had just walked out, which in effect they had! Fortunately it survived long enough for preservation enthusiasts, then virtually an unknown breed, to arrive and determine to save this relic of our railway heritage. The rest, as they say, is history.

By comparison, the Welsh Highland Railway (Light Railway) Company as an entity came into being by a Light Railway Order of 30 March 1922, acquiring, as of 1 January 1922, the existing North Wales Narrow Gauge Railways Company and the Portmadoc, Beddgelert & South Snowdon Railway Company. The former ran from Dinas, at a junction with the Caernarvon-Afonwen branch of the LNWR, to South Snowdon (otherwise known as Rhyd Ddu); and the latter had a series of unfinished works between Croesor Junction, 3 miles or so north-west of Portmadoc, and South Snowdon, with gaps north and south of Beddgelert. The company did not prosper and a Receiver was appointed on 5 March 1927!

The NWNGR was conceived as a direct result of the success of the FR in introducing steam traction to its railway and the goods and passenger traffic carried thereafter. Not surprisingly, with the Board including Livingston Thompson and Charles Spooner, respectively Chairman and Engineer of the FR, the gauge was copied and the company was incorporated on 6 August 1872. Financial problems arose right from early days and the original planned line was never built, but a route from Dinas to Snowdon was opened progressively between 1877 and 1881. Further south the story of the railway - eventually the PB&SSR - is like a play with a constantly changing plot and list of characters and, therefore, perhaps not entirely surprisingly, no complete route had been finished by the time of the inauguration of the WHR in 1922.

A physical link with the FR was secured after 1923, with completion of the route to Portmadoc and access to Harbour Station (then known as Portmadoc Old) by way of the old Croesor Tramway trackbed, but another link had been indirectly forged from 1877, when the NWNGR took delivery of two Robert Fairlie-designed locomotives, but this time 'singles' as opposed to the double-ended examples on the FR.

The young WHR was initially acutely short of motive power and borrowed from the FR, there being direct running between the two railways, with FR engines reaching right to Dinas. Traffic receipts never rose to levels anticipated or needed, however, and after the appointment of the Receiver, the health of the railway declined. A leasing to the FR in 1934 led to that railway attempting to drum up business by repainting stations and the locomotive *Russell* in light green, re-opening the Dinas refreshment room, providing a station mistress in national costume at Beddgelert, and changing the name of Nantmor station to Aberglaslyn, but any upturn in business was short-lived. The position was not helped by Beddgelert becoming effectively a frontier town, with all trains terminating there, forcing travellers for the whole length to change trains. The end finally came in September 1936 for passengers, and June 1937 for freight, after which the railway was abandoned, in much the same way as the FR ten years later. Dismantled during the war years, that is how the situation has remained ever since.

Sadly, the WHR did not live long enough to reap the benefits of enthusiasm as did the FR, but the line never died in many people's hearts and there have been plans, thoughts and schemes to resurrect the railway for many years. Now, with the initial considerations of ownership and finance surmounted, the prospects look truly exciting. This book attempts to show what has and could be achieved, and is perhaps unique among 'past and present' selections, in that there are scenes of positive and negative progress as well as complete change and promise of further development.

I have attempted wherever possible to duplicate views precisely, but this has often been obstructed, sometimes literally, by changes over the years; also the different focal lengths of the old cameras sometimes made exact copying difficult. Unless otherwise stated, all the present views were taken during the week 5-9 June 1995, and were taken by myself.

It is a historical accident that the railway was registered as Festiniog, with one 'F'; present operations use the more accurate Ffestiniog and I have copied this more modern spelling in the captions, except for those places where the original company is referred to. Similarly, the name Portmadoc was changed around 1974 to Porthmadog, and again I have used the modern version except where historically inaccurate to do so.

M. John Stretton

Tickets from the 1950s and 1990s.

THE WELSH HIGHLAND RAILWAY

Caernarvon

Caernarvon was at its height an important railway centre. Built by the London & North Western Railway, the station was the hub of lines handling traffic for this centre of local tourism and business. Reaching north there was Bangor and the North Wales main line, and south a line to Afonwen, a terminus situate by the GWR Cambrian Coast line to Pwllheli; there were branches *en route*, to Llanberis and Nantlle, and a connection at Dinas Junction with the North Wales Narrow Gauge/Welsh Highland Railway. Some of its own sense of importance can be seen in this photograph from the very early years of this century, when horses were very much the street motive power. A handsome two-horse-drawn carriage awaits its occupants by the imposing station building.

Barely recognisable as the same place, this transformation has only happened in the last few years, as Safeway built its supermarket. Links with the past are the line of the road, still heading towards Bangor, and the building in the right middle distance, although this has been substantially altered over the years. Perhaps hard to visualise, but the man about to go through the gap in the station wall on the right of the 'past' picture is roughly where the road drain is in the pavement in this shot. *Lens of Sutton/MJS*

Another view of Caernarvon in happier times. On Sunday 22 July 1962 the RCTS ran a special to Afonwen, headed by two Stanier Class '3' 2-6-2Ts, and they are seen during a water stop at the station. Much of the Victorian infrastructure on the right has survived over the succeeding 60 years or so, with the Menai Straits side of the station, to the left of the train, having undergone most change, not least the footbridge being rebuilt and losing its canopy.

Again, Safeway dominates the present scene, with nothing to immediately link the two views; the houses on the main road, seen in the background of the 'past' picture, are still there, but masked by the supermarket building. There has been talk of rebuilding the line to Bangor and it is just conceivable that the space to the left of the building could be utilised, but the way south, behind the photographer, is currently blocked by a new car park. *Gavin Morrison/MJS*

Dinas Junction

Dinas Junction station is just a few miles south of the centre of Caernarvon and was once the changing point, as the station board rather grandly (and hopefully?) announces, for 'Snowdon, Beddgelert, Portmadoc and Blaenau Ffestiniog'. Although technically possible to travel the full 35-mile length to this latter town, by NWNGR/WHR and Festiniog Railway trains, it is unlikely that this 1920s family group are to attempt what would be a trek of several hours.

While the ex-LNWR waiting room and signal box have since disappeared, the Welsh Highland goods shed, extreme left, station master's house (above the far carriage) and waiting room, on the grass-covered platform, are still extant 70 years later! However, a brick building covers the spot where the family waited, although the road overbridge and platform edges confirm the location. Hopefully the tarmac will be replaced by rails again within just a few years, when the present occupants of the site will have vacated and this location will be the first goal and temporary terminus of a re-emerging Welsh Highland Railway. *Lens of Sutton/MJS*

Left A view looking north from the road overbridge in 1934. Hunslet 2-6-2T *Russell*, in the centre distance, is just about to run round its train by the standard gauge exchange tracks, while a gentleman waits patiently at the foot of the station entrance near the wooden ticket office. Originally built as the waiting room, its function was swapped with the brick building behind it sometime around 1923.

It is now almost impossible to walk down the approach ramp to the station (left) due to the undergrowth, and only the ex-station master's house (right) gives the link to the past. The tree by the car, which is parked by the site of the wooden ticket office, hides the Welsh Highland goods shed, but evidence of development and enlargement of the site can be seen to the right of this scene in 1995. *P. M. Gates, WHS collection/MJS*

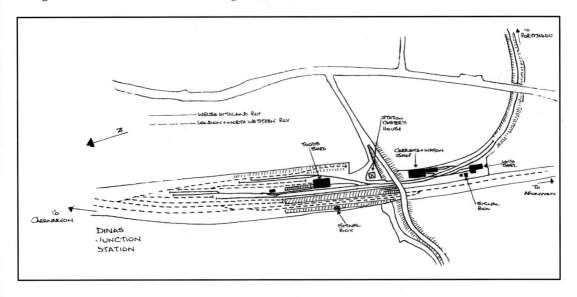

Sketch map of Dinas Junction.

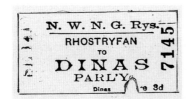

Two Welsh Highland tickets and a rare NWNGR example.

The same view as in the previous photographs, but this time looking from beneath the bridge towards the goods shed on 8 August 1935. On the left is a train in the station, and on the right a passenger carriage rests on the approach track to the coal sidings. Note the yellow brickwork on the bridge arch; this somewhat lavatorially coloured brick was a feature of the architecture of the NWNGR.

Sixty years later the attractive stone retaining walls have been replaced by concrete panels, the tracks have gone, gates have been fitted to protect industrial units, and the hedge immediately through the arch keeps prying eyes from the ex-station master's house. The wall of the goods shed can just be seen sprouting from the bonnet of the car. *H. F. Wheeller, R. S. Carpenter collection/MJS*

The view from the same bridge looking south in 1934. The LNWR standard gauge track on the right heads towards Afonwen, while the single-track WHR running line swings sharply left towards Tryfan Junction, behind the tree and white building on the extreme left to run under the road to Caernarvon. The buildings on the left are the carriage sheds, with the dark construction beside the signal box being the engine shed, with a sand store and water tower immediately to its left.

By 1995 the trees have grown, almost obliterating the church spire, which can still just be seen above the industrial units. The old engine shed is still there, now modified, but nothing else, not even the trackbed, remains. To re-create a railway to Caernarvon here, it is proposed to use the original route from the south as far as the engine shed, then run straight ahead to access the old LNWR trackbed behind the trees on the right, before swinging north through the old station site. *P. M. Gates, WHS collection/MJS*

Tryfan Junction to South Snowdon

Two miles out from Dinas, Tryfan Junction station saw a maximum running speed of 4 mph; if the trackwork was in anything like this condition, uncared for and overgrown in 1941, five years after closure, then it is hardly surprising! The station had ceased to be a junction for passenger services to Bryngwyn in 1916, and was demoted to halt status in 1934, but seven years on still proudly retains its nameboard. With wagons from the demolition train on the right, however, the end is nigh!

Amazingly enough, the young lady is standing in exactly the same spot as the lone visitor in 1941! The building still stands, just, amongst the trees, albeit without a roof and with some of the stone walling having collapsed, but it is hardly conceivable that this was once a railway station! Having to indulge in some judicious pruning to even obtain this shot, this area would make a superb project for adoption by a section of Welsh Highland volunteers, where signs of progress could very quickly be seen. *J. F. Bolton, WHS collection/MJS*

A little further east is Waenfawr. It is entirely fitting that the Ffestiniog should be linked with the Welsh Highland preservation movement, as in the early days of the NWNGR engines of the FR ran through to Dinas Junction. The FR's *Palmerston* is seen arriving at Waenfawr with a northbound train in 1924. There seem to be few passengers, the notice board is blank and the signal box was empty at this date, but the driver seems keen to have his presence recorded!

Planned to be the southern terminus of the renovated line from Caernarvon for a period, while work continues further south, it will be a relatively simple matter to re-lay the loop line, for run-round facilities, and to rebuild the station itself. The pub, whose garden can be seen on the right, will no doubt enjoy the new traffic! In 1995 there is no sign on the ground of the site of the signal box, but most of the houses remain on the hillside, the view of which is little changed over 70 years. *Real Photographs, WHS collection/MJS*

Two miles further south, on the road to Porthmadog, is the delightful Vale of Bettws Garmon, with the Afon Gwyrfai running alongside and criss-crossing the road. The main station was at Bettws Garmon itself, where in the early years of the North Wales Narrow Gauge Railway much revenue was earned through an adjacent siding for the transhipment of iron ore. One mile south of this a Halt was provided for Plas-y-nant, situated up a small side road towards an abandoned quarry. Single-Fairlie *Moel Tryfan* is seen approaching the very rudimentary station, once more crossing the river as it heads south with a rake of NWNGR stock, in the early 1890s. In the background is Mynydd Mawr, sometimes known as Elephant Mountain, although not recorded as such on maps of the area.

While little of the above view changed while the WHR still ran, the ravages of time and progress make it difficult to exactly replicate the earlier shot. There are three mountains in the area that look similar and it takes some detective work to establish the precise location, when the growth of the spindly trees of 1895, seen a century later, threatens to block the entire view. The single-span bridge is still extant amongst the trees, although now rather treacherous to pass over, and the trackbed is intact, stretching across the valley floor towards the elephant's ear. *A. E. Rimmer, WHS collection/MJS*

South Snowdon station was just over 9 miles from Dinas Junction, and was one of the more important along the route, having a passing loop and a coal siding. Under the operations of the NWNGR, it was the southern terminus of the line from Dinas and known purely as Snowdon; the addition of 'South' was made in October 1923 by the WHR (which had taken over the line on 1 January 1922) to denote that the south face of the mountain could be seen from its platform. During the ownership of the NWNGR, Single-Fairlie *Moel Tryfan* enters the station with a southbound train, past the building proudly displaying 'Refreshment Room' on its roof. Beverages seem to have been important, judging by the two signs for 'Everybody's Tea, 2/- lb.', while the other enamel signs, together with the dress of the waiting passengers, are fascinating. The wagon in the foreground is also interesting, as no sidings at this point are shown on any station plans!

While it may not appear as the same location, the white house on the extreme right of the earlier photograph is still in use, but now completely hidden from view behind the tremendous growth of trees; the outline of the hills and mountains in the background is also altered by tree growth. The site, now known as Rhyd Ddu, is a public car park and popular picnic spot, but the line of the trackbed is still clear and largely unfettered. *WHS/MJS*

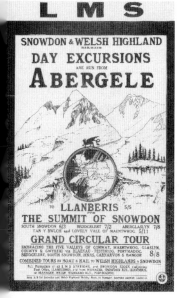

Beddgelert

For long a changing point for passengers to and from both Porthmadog and Dinas Junction, after the FR ceased to negotiate the whole route, Beddgelert was an important point, with often more activity than at most other places along the route. The facilities, especially for passengers, were limited to put it mildly, there being an open-fronted waiting room measuring 40 ft by 12 ft, with one end partitioned off as an office, but, incredibly, the provision of a bookstall in a separate building! For the loco operations, there was a water tower, an inspection/ash pit, and a goods shed with siding. The tower is in use here, replenishing *Russell* ready for a run up the line to Dinas Junction in the early 1930s, while the guard chats to a gentleman resting easily on his bicycle.

Remarkably, 60 years on, the base of the tower still stands, awaiting possible re-use with the re-establishment of the railway, and the loco pit is in good condition to its right, but elsewhere the railway infrastructure has gone, with the sole exception of the concrete base of the waiting room, just visible to the left of centre of this picture. The white house on the extreme left has had an extension over the years. *WHS/MJS*

WELSH HIGHLAND RAILWAY.
BEDDGELERT
TO
ANY STATION
Not exceeding 12 miles
Available by one Train and to one Station only
and must be given up at end of journey.
1 CYCLE -- 9d. PAID.

No 12 *Russell* is seen again, on 8 August 1935, having just arrived at Beddgelert from Dinas, and is resting while its complement of passengers discuss their next moves. Its final condition, after the FR amended the original lines by trimming cab, dome and chimney, is clearly seen, as is the corrugated-iron waiting room.

By June 1995 the hills behind have changed little, but on the ground only that concrete base for the waiting room can still be seen, just right of centre. This area, high above the town, is still untouched and it would present little problem to replace the railway, no doubt bringing welcome trade to the town and the Royal Goat Hotel just below it. *H. F. Wheeller/MJS*

This is the view of Beddgelert station looking north from the footpath leading up from the Royal Goat Hotel, not long after construction of the railway. The presence of two lorries, the nearest being a delightful Model T of a local coal merchant, either means a train is due, or that the drivers have great hopes!. The newness of construction can be judged by the bare rocks on the cutting sides, whereas, by June 1995, Nature has made a bold advance!

Incredibly this is the same vantage point, and on this day there was still track in the cutting, albeit that laid some years before by the WHR (1964) Co. It is difficult, if not impossible, to discern even the outline of the right-hand embankment, and this stretch will need concerted attention before the line can be re-opened.
F. Frith & Co Ltd, National Library of Wales Collection/MJS

The 75 ft span Bryn-y-Felin bridge straddles the Afon Glaslyn some half-mile south of Beddgelert, taking the railway away from more open, pasture land to the foot of the hills. In this undated view, probably soon after opening, the river is in full (spring?) flood, and the stone retaining wall and abutments supporting the sturdy girder bridge are obviously needed.

The strength of those abutments and the bridge have meant that the footpath, created on the trackbed, has been able to cross the river with little in the way of adaptation. In 1995 the stone wall has gone and the railway embankments on either side of the bridge have levelled out somewhat, giving walkers easier access to the main path from connected walks. *Real Photographs, WHS/MJS*

Looking the other way from the rocky outcrop seen in the previous picture, *Russell* heads south towards the Aberglaslyn Pass over the track for Bryn-y-Felin Farm, guarded by gates, on a special run in the early 1930s. A van provides solitary road competition on the re-aligned A487.

Despite the lack of tracks for nearly 60 years, the road alignment has not changed and a modern-day van negotiates the bend of the road embankment in June 1995. The farm track has become a footpath and the vegetation has grown, but the scene is instantly recognisable and the vantage point will make for superb photographic opportunities when the railway returns. *Photomatic, WHS/MJS*

Aberglaslyn Pass and Nantmor

In the Aberglaslyn Pass, the nature of the outcrops and the tunnelling into the side of Craig-y-llan necessary to accommodate the stretch of line running alongside the River Glaslyn, meant that much effort was required to secure the route of the line, especially as it was declared that there be at least 6 feet on either side of the centre line of the track. It was said that trains could travel through with coach doors open without problem, but the engineers were helped by the granite structure of the rock and the attendant lack of need for tunnel lining. In this view, looking south on 8 August 1935, the support for the telephone wires can be seen in the tunnel roof.

Despite the unchecked growth of flora over 60 years, the virtually unchanged contours of the tunnels are testament to the strength of the rock, and even the remains of the telephone pole stick hangs from the roof. The walkers are seated on the base of a machine gun emplacement, placed there during the war - one wonders how many Germans were expected through the Pass! *H. F. Wheeller/MJS*

The narrowing of the gorge through which the Glaslyn flows can be clearly seen in this view from higher up, leading to the blasting of the longest tunnel - the hole in the middle distance accessing 300 yards of darkness. The bareness of rock and the lack of road traffic conspire to create a deserted feeling as Baldwin 4-6-0 No 590 heads north for Beddgelert through the Pass in 1925.

That same gun emplacement is seen again on the trackbed, but now the scene is far more welcoming, with prodigious growth of bushes and trees; the road also now sees considerably more traffic! Note that many of the rocks in the river are in the same place as 70 years earlier! *F. Frith & Co Ltd, WHS/MJS*

Nantmor Cutting is at the southern end of the tunnels, the track running firstly on to an embankment, over the final fall of Cwm Bychan, then into a deep cleft in an outcrop of rock. On 8 August 1935 the Baldwin again works northwards, up the prevailing 1 in 40 gradient, with a short mixed train including a Pickering-built coach next to the gentleman lazily resting on the platelayers trolley at the rear, seemingly blissfully unaware of any health and safety aspects, despite it only being attached by rope!

Only the ferns and the line of the fence are recognisable in this view, as the intervening years have allowed unchecked advance of surrounding vegetation, blocking out even the skyline. The trackbed remains, however.
H. F. Wheeller/MJS

The same train draws slowly towards the tunnel, rounding the bend through the rock cutting, with the two men (one being hidden in the previous picture) still safely aboard. Mountain ranges stand proudly as a backdrop, while behind the photographer is Nantmor station, once the proud possessor of a siding and coal yard.

The mountains have disappeared from view and only the trackbed gives any clue, in June 1995, to the existence of a past railway. *H. F. Wheeller/MJS*

Portmadoc

When it was built, the WHR crossed the GWR on the flat on its approach to Portmadoc, as can be seen here. Prior to the Grouping of 1923 the then Cambrian Railways had a hut 'manned' by a woman with a flag! The incoming GWR, being the larger and more powerful organisation compared with the WHR, took priority and installed a small signal box, which, together with stop boards on either side on the WHR alignment, gave control over access. This new box is seen not long after completion in 1923; the water tower on the other side of the gates - which were to keep animals off the GWR! - is also new.

In this 1995 view the only building left to identify the position is the Tabernacle Chapel in the middle distance, seen just above the right-hand gate post in the 'past' picture. Here Dr Thomas David Edwards, composer of the well-known hymn 'Rhyd y Groes', was organist during the 1920s; his grandson, Paul Davies, is a fireman on the current FR! *Real Photographs, WHS/MJS*

Portmadoc New was the name given to the WHR station when it was opened at this point in 1923. Shortly after opening, the driver and guard of a southbound train, hauled by FR locomotive *Merddin Emrys*, pose for the camera, while the onlookers have climbed the steps from the station building at a lower level. The long building to the left is the refreshment room, and the GWR signal box can be seen just to the right of a Dinas-bound train.

The hills are the same and the water tower base remains in 1995 (the tank is seen in the 'past' picture just to the left of the rear of the Dinas-bound train), but all else has changed, even to the alignment of the loop line having been fenced off and virtually obliterated. The 1923 station, having initially taken over from Harbour station, was abandoned after only five years or so, due to operational problems with the GWR over the crossing - it is to be hoped that the re-introduced railway will have better luck with Railtrack! *Real Photographs, WHS/MJS*

WELSH HIGHLAND RAILWAY.
PRIVILEGE TICKET
Issued in exchange for P.T. order at one
fourth ordinary single fare and subject to conditions on the back hereof.

PORTMADOC

to

FIRST CLASS

473

The train of 8 August 1935, seen at Nantmor on pages 29 and 30, is here captured earlier in the day, heading away from Harbour station, across High Street and about to enter Madoc Street, where it will run on the former Croesor Tramway route towards New Station. Such was the traffic at this date that the passage of a train across the tarmac gave little disruption to road business, and the gentle sight of the lone cyclist gives an added air of peace and tranquillity long since gone from the area.

Some of the hustle and bustle of present-day Porthmadog (as it is now known) can be judged from this view. The spacious road and delightful garden wall have given way to a sharper corner and the entrance to a filling station, traffic is much more prolific and the Maenofferen Quarry Office, on the far corner of Madoc Street, has become a gift shop. *H. F. Wheeller/MJS*

Looking at the entrance to Madoc Street from a slightly different vantage point, on 8 July 1936, we see *Russell* passing the Rhosydd Quarry Office (right) with a train nearly at its Harbour station destination. The Crosville bus stop hangs at a jaunty angle from the tree, announcing stops by request, but it is hard to see where intending passengers for this competition to the railway should actually stand while waiting!

The two ex-quarry offices are both still extant, but now under different guises - the ex-Rhosydd partly as an accommodation booking office - and the peace and quiet has gone; even the gift shop is encouraging young travellers to think road rather than rail! *S. W. Baker, WHS/MJS*

The Britannia Bridge, over the same Afon Glaslyn that has run down from Beddgelert, has changed more than once in its lifetime, and in 1923 was widened and strengthened to more ably accommodate the trains. Thirteen years on, in 1936, Baldwin No 590 manoeuvres its way gingerly over the bridge towards Harbour station with an unusual mixed train. The young boys watch the concerned concentration of the railman with interest, while a classic soft-top car heads for the town centre. Note the Oakeley name on the signboard; owners of one of the most successful slate businesses of its time, the family built Plas Tan-y-Bwlch, which still stands in its magnificent grounds and which is served by Plas Halt on the preserved FR.

The bridge has again seen much attention in the ensuing 59 years, and the ex-slate wharf area has been developed, now being occupied by Y Ganolfan Hall and a small shopping complex. *E. R. Morten/MJS*

On 5 September 1958, in a period when the Welsh language was making strides to re-establish itself, the FR's first restored loco, the 1863-built *Prince*, approaches Britannia Bridge, past the old toll house, the driver anxiously looking ahead to ensure no problems with his train of flats over the old trackwork.

In 1995 the old toll house remains, still with the same slate frontage, but with its chimneys and ridge tiles changed and its residents protected by a wooden fence; the building on the other side of the road, however, has gone. The trackbed of *Prince*'s train can be judged from the different paving and the pedestrian walkway across the bridge, but for any restoration of the railway the track is likely to occupy the toll house side of the **bridge.** *M. Dean, Hefin Williams collection/MJS*

THE FFESTINIOG RAILWAY

Portmadoc

Portmadoc Harbour station, known as Portmadoc Old during the time of the WHR, is the western-most point of the Ffestiniog Railway and the place where the greatest emphasis has been made, since renaissance of the railway in the mid-1950s, to welcome and entertain the public. At restoration there was much to be done to merely allow trains to function, and the railway had a distinctly run-down air, as the old operation had effectively been 'switched off' in 1946 and left to rot thereafter. For the first 20 years the major effort was concentrated on getting the railway up and running and extending the operational mileage; consequently much of the infrastructure retained the aura of the past, as seen here on Thursday 10 July 1969, with *Earl of Merioneth* pausing to take water prior to running round its train for another journey up the line.

As can be seen from the 1995 view, much changed during the next 25 years. The station buildings have been transformed, with additions of new buildings and awnings fitted to the platform elevation; the fencing has been completely renewed and the fuelling area generally cleaned up; the water tank has grown somewhat; and oil now rules, compared to the need for coal on site in 1969. Also, the engines themselves now have a much more cared-for appearance, and *Merddin Emrys*, sister (or should that be brother?) to the *Earl*, looks magnificent in its maroon livery. FR servants David Black and Colin Dukes look somewhat dubious as to their part in the story! *Horace Gamble/MJS*

Left From the early days of the restored railway, the Double-Fairlie locomotives, superb machines and a particular feature of the FR, have been the mainstay of operations. Here, in August 1959, No 3 *Taliesin* has arrived with a service from Tan-y-Bwlch, then the northern terminus.

In the 1990s the public are intrigued and fascinated by history re-enacted or re-created, but they also demand creature comforts. The success of the FR in providing this can be judged from this view showing the tidiness of the station environs, the smartness of *Merddin Emrys* and the amenities added by the railway. The original buildings are still extant, but now there are new buildings, housing the shop and cafe, between those old ones and the ex-goods shed (now the museum), seen above the far coach. The provision of new purpose-built coaching stock, seen here, has also enhanced the traveller's comfort. *J. F. Clay/MJS*

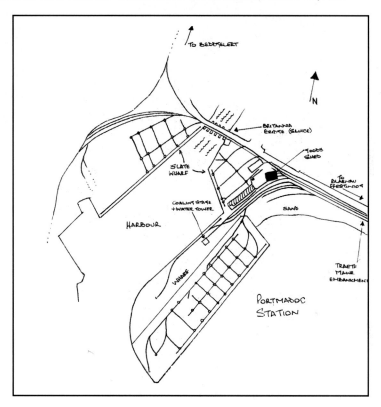

Sketch map of Portmadoc Harbour station.

FESTINIOG RAILWAY.

NOTICE IS HEREBY GIVEN THAT

SMOKING IS NOT ALLOWED

IN THE

STATION WAITING ROOMS.

BY ORDER.

PORTMADOC,
December 1st, 1896.

Printed by LLOYD & SON, 125, High Street, Portmadoc.

The date is 6 September 1955 and the new railway is still in its infancy, with much work to be done by the early volunteers. The newly revitalised *Prince*, standing by the booking office, is also in a new infancy, for, although having been built in 1863, a new boiler had been ordered during the war and it was only fitted in 1955, with the locomotive entering service on 5 August, just a month before this view.

The loco is the same but there has been dramatic change. There are many detail differences in *Prince*'s appearance, the trackwork has been cleared and in places realigned, but the aforementioned developments for creature comforts are well displayed, with the railway now possessing a well-cared-for and welcoming appearance. The length of trains has also increased over the years, to cater for the influx of visitors, but history has not been abandoned and the vintage set, seen here, is ever popular, enabling passengers to sample some of the travel conditions of the past. *P. B. Whitehouse/MJS*

A poster timetable from 1956.

Compare this shot, taken on a wet day in July 1965, with that opposite, and the first fruits of restoration are clear. *Prince* once again stands in the station platform, with driver Bill Hoole awaiting the 'right away', but now seats have been provided for waiting passengers, as well as a 'Ladies Room', and a fence looks to have been newly erected. The sign warns visitors that it would not be advisable to visit the railway on Sundays!

Drivers obviously take their roles seriously, judging by the 1995 version, Colin Dukes taking a keen interest in the gentleman closely inspecting *Prince*. Again, the cosmetic improvements of Harbour station are apparent (and plenty of seats this time!), as is the re-alignment of the track over the intervening 30 years; the many detail differences on *Prince* can also be picked out. *Terry Gough/MJS*

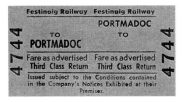

As well as the railway, the town of Portmadoc has also seen much change over the years, not least at the east end of town. Sitting between Britannia Terrace and the mile-long Cob, the Britannia Foundry once gave much gainful employment to the Victorian town, and even cast items for the railway, but it fell into disuse in 1965. In the late 1960s *Earl of Merioneth* backs on to its train, watched by potential passengers and the fireman of *Blanche*.

In the late 1970s the foundry was demolished, making way for the erection of offices for the Inland Revenue. With them as backdrop, evidence of longer trains nowadays is the fact that *Merddin Emrys*, waiting to leave with the last train of the day, the 15.55 to Blaenau Ffestiniog, is unable to draw any closer to the station buildings, the rake of coaches occupying the whole length of the platform. *Jon Marsh/MJS*

Britannia Foundry is again seen in this 1956 view of *Prince* apparently shunting in a field and in danger of being watered, in view of the dog having its leg raised! The extent of clearance work to be done by the early volunteers can be seen.

Once more the achievements of those, and subsequent, volunteers can clearly be judged, with the view hardly being recognisable as the same vantage point. Track realignment has meant that *Prince* cannot stand on the same spot as before, but the area is still used to rest between duties. Note the many differences in the loco's tender over the years, not least occasioned by the alterations for oil-firing. *Norman Keen/MJS*

In the days of the pre-preservation, the line joining the FR and the WHR, by way of the Britannia Bridge, entered Harbour station roughly between the second and third coaches in this view. This connection was lifted in 1958, but the short spur to the goods shed still remained and can be seen behind the train in this view of *Prince* engaging in a spot of shunting in July 1965. Note the proliferation of television aerials on the houses of Britannia Terrace!

Progress is evident everywhere in this view. The trackwork has of necessity been radically altered to cope with the increased demands of the operating department, and this has included the removal of that spur to the goods shed. Britannia Foundry has gone, and, in a strange twist of progress, so have the vast majority of those aerials! *Terry Gough/MJS*

Boston Lodge

Pen Cob Halt was situated by the end coaches of the 2.30 pm Portmadoc to Tan-y-Bwlch train, seen here leaving the Cob hauled by Double-Fairlie *Taliesin* on 29 June 1960. Opened as a stopping point in the very early days of the restored railway, its location was not ideal, and with the progression of the railway northwards it was withdrawn from use between 1956 and 1958.

This is not exactly the same view, since the vantage point of 1960 has been swept away in subsequent developments within Boston Lodge. The location is the same, however, and the engine is another Double-Fairlie, this time *Merddin Emrys*, by now oil-fired, doing away with the stacks of coal seen on *Taliesin*'s tank tops. The 15.55 Porthmadog-Blaenau Ffestiniog service turns into Boston Lodge curve, with fireman Paul Davies concentrating on his duties. *Terry Gough/MJS*

Boston Lodge is the site of both the railway's engine shed and Works, as well as providing storage for some of the coaching stock. The Works have achieved great things for the railway over the years, not least the building of four Double-Fairlies. Coal firing on railways has always been very labour intensive and dirty, and in preservation days the position is no different; on 25 August 1969 *Earl of Merioneth* receives tender loving care from volunteers preparing it for its next turn.

By comparison, the view at the same point in June 1995 is spotlessly clean! Gone is the total reliance on coal; also absent is the foundry chimney, together with its attendant buildings. New ones have been erected, existing ones have been extended and the track has been realigned. *Merddin Emrys* runs into the yard for attention after a hard day's work. *John Hunt/MJS*

FESTINIOG & WELSH HIGHLAND RLYS.

FOR REPAIRS

From ....
To ....
Date ....
Defects ....

Any unauthorised person removing this Card from the Vehicle to which it has been attached will render himself liable to Criminal Prosecution.

Looking in the opposite direction during the Centenary Weekend in 1963, *Merddin Emrys* and *Prince* stand on that same line, while *Linda* rests as her tender is replenished with coal. In the background is the 'long shed' into which the engines would repair after duties.

Without the 'long shed' as backdrop - it was demolished in 1988 - the ambience of the scene is totally different, with the view towards Tremadoc Bay being wide open. The right-hand gate pillar was removed earlier to give clearer access, but the left-hand building wall still remains and the pit is still in use, with *Merddin Emrys* resting over it, having completed its day's duties. *Jon Marsh/MJS*

When the volunteers first came on to the railway, the track was home to quantities of sand from the estuary, spread out behind the photographer, but by the time of this view, 6 September 1955, nature was being tamed and trains could sweep round Boston Lodge curve off the Cob and begin the long climb up the line. Two youthful volunteers mount guard as *Prince* hauls its short load past the ex-staff cottages, which used to have stables in front of them, and the high wooden fence, demolished in 1958.

Over the 40 intervening years much has been achieved in presenting a more professional face to the public, which is also now privy to a much clearer view of the Works yard on the right as the trains sweep round the curve. Evidence of the longer trains is again obvious, as *Prince* heads north, together with certain structural alterations and a liberal amount of paint on the cottage walls; even the road seems to have been widened since 1955. *P. B. Whitehouse/MJS*

Minfordd

Minffordd is the first main station out of Porthmadog and it returned to public timetabled operation on 19 May 1956. Brought on loan from Penrhyn Quarry earlier in the year, *Linda*, running as in the quarry without a tender, and carrying the bucket that was a trademark for so long, has her first run out on FR metals approaching the station in 1962. The line to the right, despite appearances, is not a 'down' line, but instead is the route into Minffordd yard, once the site of freight exchange with the standard gauge Cambrian Railways; the latter's tracks run under the parapet seen to the right of the second coach.

The present-day FR has never been slow in embracing technology and requirements such as Health & Safety, aware that it owes a duty to the public to present the best. Signalling and points have incorporated this, as can be seen here, as three-year-old *David Lloyd George*, built at Boston Lodge Works by the FR, approaches the station with the 12.50 Porthmadog-Blaenau Ffestiniog service. There is an extra link between these two views: the right-hand figure on the footplate of *Linda* in 1962 is none other than Evan Davies, driver of *DLG* in 1995! *Hefin Williams collection/MJS*

From a period (and world) that has long gone, and looks it, an 'up' train, hauled by an unidentified Double-Fairlie, passes a sister engine on its 'down' equivalent as it enters the platform in 1938. The fireman seems ready and alert to his duties and responsibilities as he leans nonchalantly from the cab, but both he and the guard of the down train closely watch the passenger on the right who appears to be about to court disaster by walking into the path of the incoming train!

By 1995 the lamp has been restored to the iron bracket, although teas are no longer dispensed, and the toilets, left, have undergone a change of use. The ramp down to the BR station is still in use, seen just to the left of the engine, and a modern tourist watches as fireman Andrew Morris, with single-line token in his left hand, appears to be pointing to some aspect of his charge. *David Lloyd George* again heads the 12.50 service from Porthmadog.
Ken Weaver/MJS

Judging by the number of people waiting, this could be rush-hour at Minffordd! On 14 June 1961 volunteers pose appropriately for the camera. Left to right: Ron Lester, who was PW Foreman; Alan Skellern, still with the railway in the S&T department; John Halsall, who is now retired and lives in a Boston Lodge cottage; and the late Paul Dukes, who was Works Manager - his son Colin carries on the family tradition by being a driver on the railway. Note the ornate lamp bracket in the centre, and the various posters showing places of interest, but strangely advertising other railways!

The posters wall has now been buried behind the block instrument control box, the beams of the waiting shelter roof have been covered and the lamp bracket has sadly gone, illumination now provided by a less than attractive modern version. Otherwise, the station is much as before, albeit cleaner, with a less 'lived in' appearance, as a sole, American, visitor waits for the trains on 4 June 1995. *Hefin Williams collection/MJS*

Another view of the station, with the lamp brackets seen in the previous pictures again visible, as *Taliesin* enters from the north with the 3.35 pm Tan-y-Bwlch to Portmadoc train on 6 July 1960. Although cleared and sufficiently ballasted, the left-hand track was not in constant use for passenger trains, and the old 'down' platform is subject to the whims of Nature.

By contrast, as the 14.05 Blaenau Ffestiniog-Porthmadog train slows into the station, with fireman Paul Davies keeping look-out ahead from the cab of *Merddin Emrys*, the view in June 1995 shows just what can be done to give an image of a successful railway. The buildings have been restored, re-roofed, re-painted; the platforms have been reinstated and raised; the gardens are now lovingly tended; the track is well cared for; and the trains eminently look the part. *Terry Gough/MJS*

Penrhyn

Only 3 miles or so from Porthmadog, but already substantially above sea level, Penrhyn was in the process of reverting to nature when the preservationists first came to restore the line. Passengers finally got to ride to the station from 30 March 1957, when it became the northern terminus, with a loop line installed using track from the Minffordd area. In 1963 the loop is still in use, with the line now being open on to Tan-y-Bwlch; in the summer of that year Simplex *Mary Ann*, with 'headboard', and 2-4-0 diesel *Moelwyn*, substitute for a failed steam engine on a northbound service.

What a transformation! The old station buildings have been completely renovated by volunteers and are now occupied as a hostel for their use when working on the railway; the initial work was done between 1967 and 1971, followed by a further renovation in 1987. A platform has been expertly laid in the last few years, again by volunteers, resulting in the station deservedly winning an award. *Conway Castle* approaches the platform on the sole remaining running line, with the first train of the day, the 09.40 Porthmadog-Blaenau Ffestiniog.

Hefin Williams collection/MJS

A view from a train! In the summer of 1936 an unidentified Double-Fairlie (possibly *Taliesin*) leaves Penrhyn station and approaches the level crossing in a blanket of steam, watched by a railway worker (track ganger?) and postman taking time out from his rounds.

Although obviously the same place, there have been some major changes over the years. The growth of trees has all but obliterated the houses seen in the middle distance in 1936, whereas the clearance of some on the left has opened the way for others to be seen; the road appears to have been widened, straightened and raised; the crossing keeper's box has shrunk over the years; and the house on the right has received cosmetic alterations to its chimneys and roof-line. Its wall has also seen alteration, but the habit of train-watching still seems to be alive and well! *Martin Cook collection/MJS*

Since the railway was reopened beyond Penrhyn, the road crossing has been regularly manned in the old tradition; it is perhaps fortunate that the road is not the busiest through the town! In 1961 Double-Fairlie *Earl of Merioneth* is seen heading a down train between the gates, its fireman checking the guard, and the scene is watched over by the white house on the hill - named 'Talgarth' after the village near Brecon from where William Maddocks's wife came - apparently lord of all it surveys!

That explosion of greenery mentioned opposite is more obvious here. The white house and other later buildings nearby are hidden, and to the right the dry stone embankment is now largely hidden by the trees. While the crossing gates are still of the same design, they are now much smarter than previously and more traffic is held up as *David Lloyd George* heads south, with fireman Andrew Morris checking the photographer. *John Hunt/MJS*

55

Immediately over the crossing the trains curve round and over the stone embankment mentioned on the previous page. On a wet day in the late spring of 1970 *Merddin Emrys* appears to have a few leaking joints as it heads north towards Tan-y-Bwlch.

Thankfully, 4 June 1995 was drier as *Merddin Emrys* again, now in very smart maroon livery, heads the last 'up' train of the day, the 15.55 Porthmadog-Blaenau Ffestiniog. The houses are little changed over the years, but those trees have grown and the railway has installed warning notices for drivers of 'down' trains; driver Colin Dukes has his gaze fixed on other things, however! *Jon Marsh/MJS*

Just five months after the railway restored services to Tan-y-Bwlch, it already looks part of the scenery, as *Taliesin* slows for Penrhyn station with a 'down' train, past a smart-looking Ford waiting patiently, on 1 September 1958. Note that at this time both gates on the north side of the road were operated, as opposed to only one as seen earlier.

Due to the growth of vegetation and residential development, it is now difficult to replicate the 'past' view, but not impossible, as can be judged from the sight of *David Lloyd George* heading south with the 17.15 ex-Blaenau Ffestiniog service. Note just one gate being closed, and the dramatic development of the town of Penrhyn in the valley, not least the industrial units. *D. H. Wilson/MJS*

Tan-y-Bwlch

The original Festiniog Railway was opened in 1836, for the transportation of slate from Blaenau Ffestiniog down the ruling gradient to the wharves and waiting boats at Portmadoc. As already mentioned on page 35, the owner of one of the most successful slate mines was William Oakeley, and he built the family home on a hillside over-looking Maentwrog, just to the south of Tan-y-Bwlch. With the railway running high on an embankment above the house named 'Plas Tan-y-Bwlch', it was not surprising that he had a private station, 'Plas Private', installed for the

family use. A new station, 'Plas Halt', not on the site of 'Private', was opened on 1 June 1963 by the preservationists, initially with min-imal facilities, as can be seen from this view of *Earl of Merioneth* heading northwards past the site on 4 April 1969.

An old quarrymen's carriage body had been placed there some time previously as a PW hut, but this eventually gave way, in 1989, to a slightly more substantial and attractive stone building, seen here to the right of *David Lloyd George* on the 13.50 Porthmadog-Blaenau Ffestiniog in June 1995. Again a link between the two views is Evan Davies, who is the driver seen in both pictures - ready for a long-service medal?
John Hunt/MJS

Tan-y-Bwlch was for a long time the terminus of the restored railway, being re-opened on 5 April 1958 and not seeing through trains until a decade later. Once boasting a goods shed, with sidings, a booking office and a station mistress's house, the goods shed and sidings can still be seen on 27 June 1960 as *Taliesin* begins a return journey southwards with the 3.35 pm to Portmadoc, over the rationalised track and pointwork laid in 1958.

It is now virtually impossible, due to rampant undergrowth, to repeat the 'past' view, unless by scaffolding or bungee rope, but on ground level this was the comparative scene in 1995. The ex-goods shed has now been converted to a cafe and extended, and the sidings have long since been lifted, providing space for picnic tables. Push-pull car 111 is at the same spot as *Taliesin* above, as it trails the first train of the day for Blaenau Ffestiniog. *Terry Gough/MJS*

FESTINIOG RAILWAY
BLAENAU FESTINIOG
TO
TANY BWLCH
EXCESS 3rd. to 2nd. Class 3d

555

During its ten-year reign as terminus, the station had a casual, relaxed atmosphere, with no restrictions on views of or access to the trains, and the whole pace was easy-going. On 30 June 1959 *Taliesin* lazily reverses to its train, having just run round, before being coupled up and made ready to haul the 3.30 pm back to Portmadoc.

By contrast, the site in the 1990s has a far more ordered appearance. *Merddin Emrys* enters the station platform (built in 1968 to coincide with the push north to Dduallt) with the last down train, the 17.15 ex-Blaenau Ffestiniog. The immaculate-looking fence had only recently been erected by volunteers, replacing a decaying version dating from 1969, and further evidence of renovation work can be seen in the smart appearance of the ex-booking office (of 1873 vintage) on the right, which was at one point threatened with demolition. The ex-station mistress's house is seen above the first coach, and the hillsides have been swamped by arboreal growth compared to the 1959 scene. *Terry Gough/MJS*

Another view of the 1873 office at Tan-y-Bwlch, still in use on 3 April 1964. Passengers are to be hauled by ex-Penrhyn Quarry *Linda*, loaned to the FR in 1962 and formally acquired by the railway one year later. The period cars, parked anywhere, and the lack of platform and fencing (and driver!) all add to the feeling of a relaxed yesteryear.

Again, it is virtually impossible to replicate the 'past' view exactly due to undergrowth, but the footbridge, constructed during the winter of 1970/71, gives a near duplication and shows the track deviation dictated by the formation of the island platform in 1968. The catering staff are on hand to unload supplies for the station cafe from the first 'up' train of the day, hauled by *Conway Castle*, just in view at the head of the train, whilst the 'pretty' parking amplifies the more orderly ambience of the station nowadays. *John Hunt/MJS*

After the long climb up from Portmadoc, the locomotives are thirsty and the stop for water at Tan-y-Bwlch is a welcome breather for both engine and crew. The operation, as *Taliesin* is re-filled - not from the Gents! - has a timeless quality and only the human dress gives away the period as being 1966. The driver is also taking the opportunity to fill his pipe.

Despite the slightly altered angle, *Merddin Emrys* (right) is on the same spot as *Taliesin*; the old Gents and water tank is now hidden by a new and rather more substantial construction. As *Merddin Emrys* is watered, *David Lloyd George* enters the station from up the line and the fireman relinquishes the token for that section. The small garden area on the extreme right is the latest addition to the improvements constantly being provided to the station by volunteers. *Martin Cook collection/ MJS*

Immediately north of Tan-y-Bwlch is Creuau Bank, a stone embankment filling a gorge and here protected by a 10 mph speed restriction. Seen from the train, an unusual double-heading of *Moelwyn* (leading) and *Mountaineer* (train engine) set off for Dduallt in 1969.

Just over a quarter of a century later the trees are urgently pressing their claim to space, the warning not to walk the line has gone and the speed restriction is now facing 'down' trains. Fireman Paul Davies leans out to check the train as it leaves Tan-y-Bwlch and runs on to the bank. *Jon Marsh/MJS*

Dduallt

Dduallt station, which can only be reached by train or on foot, has always been in a wilderness and, despite there having been a handful of cottages in the vicinity at one time, it can never have generated much revenue. With the waters of Rhosllyn behind it, the house for the 'station master' on the left could never have been a particularly habitable dwelling! The date of this visit by diesel *Moelwyn* is not given, but is probably around 1960, when the trackwork on site was liberally coated with grass.

The station became the northern terminus in 1968 and stayed that way for nine years, while the problem of the flooding of the original route by a reservoir was tackled. The old 1836 route carried on in a straight line behind the train seen here, the 10.55 Blaenau Ffestiniog-Porthmadog, which has just travelled down the spiral 'deviation', which curves in from the right behind the trees. Driver Ian Rudd and his colleague seem happy enough as they pass the house and the former run-round loop on the right. *Hefin Williams collection/MJS*

Although trains returned to the area in the late 1960s, the FR did not wait until then before embarking on the solution to the flooding of the original route. Perhaps a little surprisingly, work did not begin at the northern end of the station platform, where the track was to spiral away clockwise, but rather the first sod was disturbed, in January 1965, on higher ground to the east. On 31 July 1965 a Schmiedag excavator is well employed, earning its keep transferring spoil into a skip that will run to the end of the short length of track, gradually extending the emerging embankment.

The transformation was complete in 1977, when trains again ran north to Tanygrisiau, and it is huge credit to the 'deviationist' volunteers that the present trackbed sits in the surroundings so naturally that it appears to have always been there. The plaque recording the start of the operations can be seen centre right, on 19 September 1995, as *Merddin Emrys* approaches with the 14.05 Blaenau Ffestiniog-Porthmadog service. The farmer's outbuildings have seen extension over the 30 years, but are now largely in disuse; the line now runs in front of these on an embankment, but nature is valiantly trying to conquer this view, together with the surrounding hinterland. *J. Ransom, FR collection/MJS*

Despite the tracks now having been lifted for some years, the farm over-bridge remains in situ, although serving no practical purpose and despite the majority of the boundary walls having been demolished. On a beautifully clear day in June 1995 the distant hills stand proudly as an aesthetic treat for walkers on this popular footpath. *Jon Marsh/MJS*

Running north of Ddduallt, the line ran through open pasture for about a mile, before plunging into the 730-yard Moelwyn Tunnel. Tracks leading to the south entrance of the tunnel were lifted in 1962 (the northern entrance having gone in 1957), but between there and Ddduallt they remained for some further years, as can be seen in this view looking in the direction of the tunnel on a dull day in the late 1960s.

As already described, the solution to the submerging of the old line beneath the waters of the Llyn Ystradau reservoir scheme was to build a new line higher up the hillside. The creation of the line, necessitating much blasting of very hard rock and a new Moelwyn Tunnel, caused a nine-year delay in re-opening beyond Dduallt to Tanygrisiau, and meant the volunteers being ferried to and from the site by rail. The site 'office', spoil siding and mechanical digger can be seen behind the train, two years after the breakthrough was made. On 29 May 1979 *Linda* heads for the new tunnel with the 12.00 Porthmadog-Tanygrisiau service.

Nature has a way of fighting back and it is already impossible to perfectly replicate the 'past' view, as the fir tree seen in the bottom left-hand corner has established too dense a canopy. The construction site has also disappeared from view and the other trees hide the far horizon, as *Linda* again heads for the tunnel mouth, this time with the 12.50 Porthmadog-Blaenau Ffestiniog train. *Tom Heavyside/MJS*

Tanygrisiau

The original approach route to Tanygrisiau initially ran across open ground after leaving the tunnel and followed the hillside contour to arrive at the station, which opened in February 1866. Later a stone viaduct replaced this first line, giving a straighter route for southern departures from the station. In this view of 29 May 1936, which shows *Merddin Emrys* heading south with a typical rake of FR stock, this structure can be seen in the background, with the train itself enjoying a route etched into the hillside. The station was off the picture to the right.

With that original approach occupied by the reservoir and its power station, the restored railway carved its new way higher up the hillside, on the other side of the rocks seen on the left of the 'past' picture, and eventually approached Tanygrisiau station above the old route, passing behind the houses seen the far side of the viaduct in 1936. These can still just be seen, on 19 September 1995, behind the Power Station Information Centre, to the right of the new Cwmorthin Bridge that spans the outflow of the waterfall. More rock has been blasted to widen the road and the wall on the right hides the bank of the reservoir, which roughly equates to the footpath in the earlier view. *R. Piercy/MJS*

North of Dduallt, the two stations of Tanygrisiau and Blaenau Ffestiniog have seen the most dramatic changes from the original railway, and the former has lost most in the way of buildings. Seen here on 15 September 1949, the station could almost be in suspended animation, being in virtually identical condition to when the railway ceased operations three years earlier; it is as if a child has merely walked away from its plaything, leaving it abandoned. Opened in 1866, and enlarged in 1879, the facilities were opulent for a small village, comprising large station offices, two goods sheds and workers' accommodation, being the result of the various quarry lines that fed into the FR both north and south of the site.

From the view of 5 August 1995 it is hard to realise that this is the same place. The rock face on the left has suffered from the attentions of the new railway, to accommodate the revised track alignment, the island platform has obliterated much of the earlier trackbed and the new signal box (yet to be operational) bears no comparison to the old station building. All that is left is one of the goods sheds, now renovated and standing to the left of the signal box, but note that the track is now at a higher elevation than of yore, due to the necessity of finding a new route into the station, following the reservoir complex swallowing the original trackbed.
R. K. Cope, R. S. Carpenter collection/MJS

Looking in the opposite direction, the 'grandeur' of the site can be judged, with the buildings still in good shape eight years after closure, on 27 October 1954. After the line ceased operations, the locals occasionally made use of the wagons left on the railway to move heavy objects, only for them to be again abandoned when finished with! Note the small turntable, to move wagons into the second goods shed to the left of the picture, and that the station sign boldly declares the village to be 'Tan-y-Grisiau', not one word as used today.

The raising of the railway can again be seen, with the current level being halfway up the old goods shed wall, some 3 feet or so higher than before. Despite its present clean appearance, there is currently not the character of the old station. *Central Electricity Authority/MJS*

73

Presenting a totally different view in 1995, with virtually everything in sight having been tidied up and/or altered for the better, the track now looks far more secure, as does the retaining wall. The house on the right has been re-roofed and those along the street re-painted; there have been additions and subtractions of trees; and the only major change that could be considered retrogressive is the disappearance of the large chapel building in the left distance. *Jon Marsh/MJS*

On the last leg of the railway's journey to Blaenau Ffestiniog, it continues the climb away from Tanygrisiau along a narrow ledge of rock, squeezed between the village street and a row of houses. Further evidence of the abandonment of the line after closure can be seen in the way that the railway's telegraph cables hang idly, in this view looking south from a footbridge to the houses in August 1970.

Groby Junction was the point where the industrial line to the Groby Granite Quarry swung eastwards, to cross Afon Barlwyd and the Tanygrisiau road before climbing to the quarry. Although long since closed, the align-

ment of the trackbed can still be discerned, veering to the left of the track between the posts in the centre of the picture, taken on a wet 28 August 1973.

The extent and value of the work undertaken on the line between 1977 and the 1982 re-opening can be judged from this view of a very professionally re-made railway, even to the provision of a proper foot crossing for the occupants of the residence that lays to the right, through the metal gate. Admittedly, sunshine helps, but the whole area now presents a much more cared-for aura. *John Hunt/MJS*

Dinas

Old Dinas Junction was 200 yards or so further on from Groby Junction, and was the site of a triple junction where, facing north-eastwards as seen here in August 1970, a line swung sharply northwards (to the left), for Nidd-y-Gigfran Quarry; the original FR 'main line' to Dinas, open from 1836 to 1899, carried straight on; and the Duffws branch (later becoming the main line) swung to the right. The boundary post of the former can just

be seen immediately past the footbridge, while the trackbed of the Dinas line can just be made out disappearing into the mighty slate pyramid.

By June 1995 the pyramid is still there, but evidence of the first two lines has gone, while the remaining FR route to Blaenau itself has received its share of professional attention. The footbridge once gave access to a mine office and short row of terraced cottages, but now all that remains is the office, altered to residential accommodation. *Jon Marsh/MJS*

As the railway crosses the Barlwyd Bridge in August 1970, evidence still remains of the second track that ran from here to just short of the old FR Exchange Station in Blaenau Ffestiniog, known as Stesion Fain, and linking with both Dinas and Glan-y-Pwll junctions on the way. In the middle distance the Welsh Slate Company's viaduct still marches across the ex-LNWR standard gauge tracks, which can just be seen running on the level left to right from there past the chapel.

The stone abutments of the bridge still serve to support trains, but the track now sits slightly higher than previously, on the 1981-constructed decking. Although the background hills are largely unaltered, the slate tip in the middle distance has gone, there has been landscaping on the left, and the growth of trees shielding the viaduct and chapel building generally gives a less harsh feel to the view. *Jon Marsh/MJS*

FESTINIOG RAILWAY
NOTICE.

It having been found that the Doors of the QUARRYMENS CARRIAGES are damaged, and that some of the Passengers jump out before the Train stops at the Stations, at great risk to themselves, and danger to the whole Train. This is to give Notice that proceedings will be taken against any one found thus breaking the Bye-Laws of the Company.

BY ORDER.

January 1st, 1895.

RHYBUDD.

Yn gymaint a bod niwed wedi ei wneyd i Ddrysau Cerbydau y Gweithwyr, a bod rhai o'r teithwyr yn neidio allan cyn i'r Gerbydres gyrhaedd yr Orsaf, er perygl iddynt eu hunain a'r teithwyr yn gyffredinol. Rhoddir rhybudd drwy hyn yr erlynir pwy bynag a ddelir yn tori Rheolau y Cwmni.

Trwy Orchymyn.

Ionawr 1af, 1895.

LLOYD & SON, PRINTERS, PORTMADOC.

Once the terminus for the old Festiniog Railway when opened in 1836, Dinas station, seen here in the late-1950s after the trackwork had finally been lifted, did not open until 1865 and only had a short operational life, closing again in 1870, subsequently to be turned over to residential occupation. The earliest line came in from the bottom left corner, as a single track at this point, but after 1899 the route came in from right bottom corner, as double track. Beyond the station is the former goods shed; to the right is the ex-LNWR Conwy Valley line, snaking away northwards from Blaenau Ffestiniog; and the Welsh Slate Company's viaduct is again seen in the distance.

The trackbeds of the two lines are still clear in this view, and there has been talk of resurrecting the 1899 (right-hand) route; it certainly would make an interesting complement to the current main line. The British Rail line still survives, despite repeated threats of closure, and this has also been the object of attention by the FR, under the Government's Rail Privatisation scheme. *Hefin Williams collection/MJS*

Glan-y-Pwll was the site of the original railway's engine shed at the northern end of the line; the building (left) had obviously seen better days when viewed on 28 August 1973, nearly a decade before trains again ran over the level crossing, the gates of which can be seen on the extreme right. Situated between the running line to Blaenau Ffestiniog and the 1899 line to Dinas, it was close to the once extensive slate sidings in the town.

Only the right-hand front pillar of the old shed remains, seen just above the digger's rear arm. The yard has been extensively re-modelled by the current FR and sees much use, as can be imagined from the stock of materials threatening to overwhelm *Harlech Castle*. *John Hunt/MJS*

The twin-gabled house seen in the last two views is that on the right of this shot, looking back to the Glan-y-Pwll yard from the road crossing. This is the scene in 1969 during the preservationists' wilderness years, the period between the line closing and again reaching Blaenau Ffestiniog. Both gate and house look long undisturbed.

Eloquently displaying just some of the achievements of the new railway, *David Lloyd George* (itself built by the railway three years before) prepares to run over the ungated, automatic light-controlled crossing with the 10.45 ex-Porthmadog train. The house is now being renovated by volunteers and may become a third hostel for the railway. 'Sharks teeth' protection has been installed for the crossing and, for future developments, there are plans to reinstate the second running line seen on the right. *Martin Cook collection/MJS*

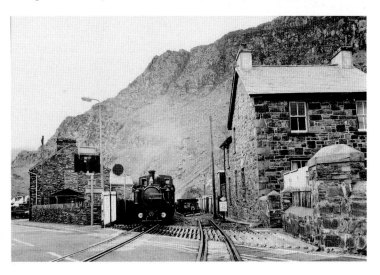

Stepping over the crossing to stand by the Glan-y-Pwll house, this is the view looking at the final yards into the town of Blaenau Ffestiniog in August 1970, the grass covering the hidden trackwork.

Again, the tremendous strides and improvements made by the current FR can be judged from this view from the same vantage point in June 1995. *Jon Marsh/MJS*

Blaenau Ffestiniog

This was the approach to the FR's Blaenau Ffestiniog Exchange Station, Stesion Fain, conveniently situated across North Western Road from the LNWR/LMS station, seen on the extreme left; both opened in 1881. Note the water tower and signal! The FR station boasted dual track until 1932, these lines continuing into the town to access that railway's Duffws terminus, the quarry lines and the slate exchange sidings situated on the far side of the standard gauge station. Seen in August 1970, the platform edging can still be made out, just to the left of the track, adjacent to the pillars that evidence an exit to the roadway; the 1962/3 road realignment to provide a by-pass for Tanygrisiau has severed the route, causing the track to come to an abrupt halt by the signboard in the middle distance.

The march forwards from Tanygrisiau, from 1977 onwards, necessitated a new approach to the town for the FR, and this was accommodated by a pre-stressed concrete box bridge being 'slotted' into the 1963 road in 1980, forethought being used to provide the facility for a second line when desired. The LMS station still stands, although closed in 1982 and now vandalised, and one pillar of the exit to North Western Road is also extant, though now a few inches shorter than previously. The North Western Hotel, just to the right of the LMS station, still open in the 1970 view, is closed and the windows boarded in this view. *Jon Marsh/MJS*

Looking back from the station towards the water tower seen in the previous picture, the Oakeley Quarry spoil tip dominates the skyline, towering over the view of the impressive station canopy, which, thankfully, was saved from demolition by being sold for use as a football stand in Manod! Seen on 16 August 1955, before the by-pass severed the site, the refreshment room two-thirds of the way along the platform has disappeared, and nature is attempting to reclaim the trackbed. The siding, caused by the 1932 severing of the previous twin track, can still be seen, and all this trackwork survived until the early 1970s.

The sharpness of the Oakeley tip has been softened by the passage of 40 years, and in June 1995 there is no outward sign that there had ever been a station here. The surrounding houses still remain, however, to satisfy that it is the same location. *Terry Gough/MJS*

Slate was, of course, the main *raison d'etre* and source of prosperity of the town of Blaenau Ffestiniog, but granite, in the form of chippings, was also a big money-earner. Both were shipped by narrow gauge to a huge area adjacent to the LMS station, bounded in the form of a flattened horseshoe by North Western Road on the south, and Llwyn-y-Gell Road and Glan-y-Pwll Road on the east and west. The yard was a maze of narrow and standard gauge lines intermingled for ease of transhipment, and with a large goods shed and ramped dock in the centre. The FR tracks, in the main, occupied the north-eastern corner of the site, with rails sweeping into sheds. A direct line from the Oakeley Quarry to the Exchange Sidings skirted the whole area. This 16 August 1955 view shows narrow and standard gauge trucks cheek-by-jowl.

Only the remaining hillside contours and housing announces this to be the same location, for, as seen in June 1995, any sign of rail linkage has been totally obliterated, the site now being occupied by, amongst others, the fire station and a bus garage. At this date some sidings still lay in the LMS yard, to the left of the photograph, but had recently been cut to prevent access! *Terry Gough/MJS*

When the FR ceased operations in 1946, the slate sidings shown in the previous picture continued to operate leased to the quarries, who used the line from the Duffws terminus to the exchange sidings until 3 November 1962. This timing coincided with the road alterations seen earlier, and BR's plans to link the previously totally separate LMS and GWR routes into the town, to provide a rail link to Trawsfynydd Nuclear Power Station. In August 1970 the line from Duffws to the exchange sidings can be seen on the left, still in situ but unused for approaching eight years, with the 'new' BR line to the right.

When the FR was close to realising the dream of returning to the town, it was obvious that the original rout

was totally unworkable, bearing in mind the BR track layout; also, with BR's plans for a new station closer to the town centre, and the FR's need for a new station site, it was decided that the two railways should 'swap sides' on this approach bottleneck. The result can be seen here as *David Lloyd George* leaves on a return journey for Porthmadog. Note that over the 25-year gap between the two photographs, the former Market Hall (left) has seen a distinct downturn in fortunes, whereas those buildings to the right of Picton bridge have enjoyed the reverse; the break in the stone wall, which once allowed the FR into a timber yard, has been plugged. *Jon Marsh/MJS*

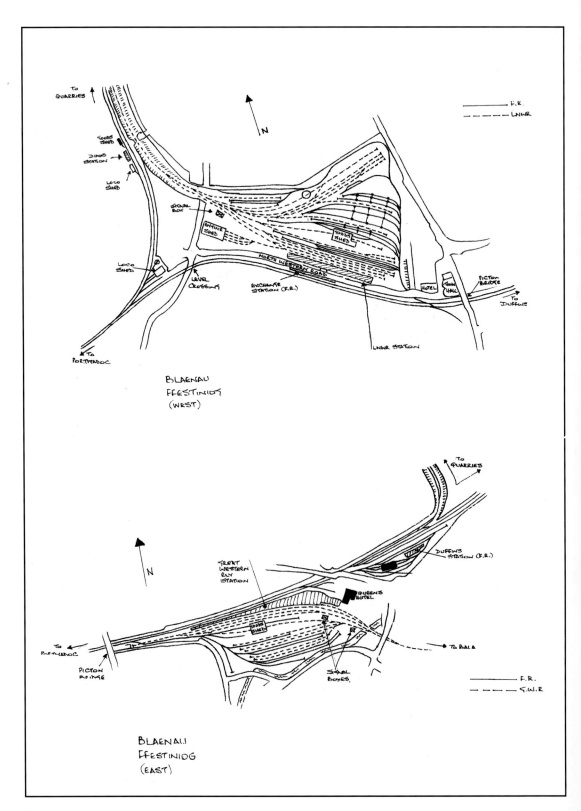

Sketch maps of the various railways and stations at Blaenau Ffestiniog.

Before the 1963 BR link, the closest the GW route into the town came to the LMS regime was this headshunt, seen on 21 April 1963 looking towards the GWR station from the Picton overbridge seen in the last two photographs. The FR's mineral line runs under the photographer, going to Duffws on the left and crossing the standard gauge, right, for transhipment purposes. Work is in hand removing the slate embankment at the top of the headshunt in conjunction with the new BR tracks; the goods yard tracks have been severed for some years, freight ending on the GW branch in January 1961.

Thirty years on there has been transformation both on and off the railway, previously overgrown and/or derelict property being cleared up and the area now presenting a far more pleasing sight. The new FR terminus can be seen in the middle distance, with the water tower to its right, and the BR station just to its left, hidden by the roof of the building at the end of the cemetery. *Hefin Williams collection/MJS*

Now approaching the centre of the town, the old FR route to Duffws is seen marching boldly forward, although by this time, 1962, it was nearing the end of its life in the hands of the quarries. Extensive track lifting has been undertaken by BR on their site, to the right, following complete closure of the ex-GWR station the previous year, and the spoil is in danger of choking the narrow gauge line. The FR track was once double under the footbridge that linked the joint station with the town, and the rails continued under the Queen's Bridge, just seen in the left distance.

Twenty years later the two railways again joined up in the town, but this time having separate structures. A school now stands on part of the ex-GWR yard to the right, with the rest of this area being occupied by the new FR station. The BR edifice is on the left, and it is hard to imagine a railway running to the left of the now whitewashed Queen's Hotel. On 6 June 1995 the FR's station seems far more popular than its big neighbour! *John Hunt/MJS*

The GWR's Blaenau Ffestiniog Central station was the terminus of the long branch from Bala. Passenger services had been terminated on 4 January 1960, and freight with effect from 30 January 1961. Perhaps not surprisingly, track reclamation has begun in this delightful view in 1962, but a start has also been made on the 'LMS/GW' connection. The picture oozes charm and atmosphere, with the period signal box, attractive awnings still extant on the platform and the ex-FR signal post, guarding that railway's station, in the mid-distance, behind the light-coloured hut.

Again, it is the hillside that gives the game away, otherwise the location is barely recognisable. Only the house seen above the station awning in 1962 can still be viewed, but even then partly hidden by the new footbridge giving access to the FR station on the left. Seemingly indelibly linked with standard gauge, the FR and LMS stations opened together in 1881, and these two new ones - the BR station is the building to the right - came almost exactly a century later, in 1982! *David Lloyd George* has just arrived with the first steam train of the day, the 10.45 ex-Porthmadog. *John Hunt/MJS*

Yet again it is only the background that gives the clue to the location. With Queen's Bridge gone, the vantage point can only now be attempted by scaling the car park wall, giving this view, in June 1995, down to the present station sites, where a Conwy Valley line DMU waits for passengers before making the return trip to Llandudno Junction. *Jon Marsh/MJS*

This is the view looking back down the ex-FR tracks from Queen's Bridge in August 1970, towards the GWR station site where the boys are playing beyond the end of the stone retaining wall. Once double-tracked here, the apparent slewing of the track is a result of track-lifting undertaken in 1922.

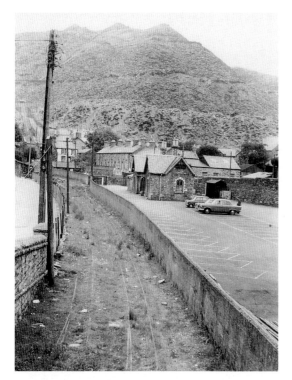

The line to the terminus at Duffws curved under Church Street, carried by Queen's Bridge, and ran into a site containing the station building, seen here, a goods shed, where the cars are, and several sidings. The station, opened in 1866, finally closed in 1931, with the goods shed being privately occupied from 1929, but the quarry slate trains still ran through the site until 1962. The tracks seen here in August 1970 would have either curved further left, to run to Maenofferen Quarry, or carried literally straight on, up the incline seen on the left, to Votty & Bowydd Quarry.

Happily, in 1995, the station building still stands, but sadly, for rail enthusiasts, for the past 25 years or so it has suffered the ignominy of being a public convenience, and it is now totally surrounded by a car park, which hosts a market on Tuesdays, as seen here. Church Street now runs on made-up ground rather than the bridge, and to attempt to replicate the 'past' view the photographer had to climb on to a slate-fashioned fountain! Note the attempt at linking the site to its past, with the slate train on its plinth; a sad epitaph, however, for a once-proud and vitally important operation. *Jon Marsh/MJS*

Timetables: 1909-1994

A **New Train** commencing February 1st, 1909, will run from Duffws *to* Portmadoc, at 7 p.m., forming a connection with Great Western train, due at Blaenau Festiniog 6.45 p.m.

(Railway timetable, left-hand panel — Cambrian Railways / L. & N.W.K. / G.W.R.)

			a.m.	a.m.	a.m.	a.m.	p.m.
Aberystwyth	...	dep.	Mon. only	8 0	10 20	1 10	
Barmouth	...	,,		9 50	12 25	2 52	
Harlech	...	,,		10 16	12 50	3 18	
Minffordd	...	arr.	5 50	10 33	1 4	3 35	
Pwllheli	...	dep.	7 45	10 30	1 25	4 0	
Criccieth	...	,,	8 12	10 56	1 50	4 30	
Minffordd	...	arr.	8 35	11 15	2 7	4 50	

Up Trains.

			Mon. exc'p. Ply. 1	Mon. only Ply. 2	3	4	5	6
			a.m	a.m	a.m	a.m	p.m	p.m
Portmadoc (for Borthygest)	dep	5 30	8 25	8 30	11 15	2 20	4 45
Minffordd	,,	5 40	8 35	8 40	11 25	2 30	4 55
Penrhyn	,,	5 45	6 0	8 45	11 30	2 35	5 0
Tan-y-Bwlch	,,	6 5	6 20	9 5	11 50	2 55	5 20
Dduallt	,,	A	A	A	A	A	A
Tan-y-Grisiau	,,	6 23	6 38	9 23	12 8	3 13	5 38
Blaenau Festiniog (L&NW) arr	6 28	6 43	9 28	12 13	3 18	5 43
Blaenau Festiniog (G.W.)	,,			9 30			5 44
Duffws	,,	6 30	6 45	9 20	12 15	3 20	5 45

Blaenau Festiniog	dep.	6 45	7 50	10 0	12 25	1 55		6 10
Bettws-y-coed	arr.	7 20	8 24	10 35	1 1	2 30		6 45
Llandudno Junction	,,	8 19	9 24	11 37	1 43	3 11		7 27
Llandudno	,,	8 20	9 25	11 37	2 2	3 40		8 0
Colwyn Bay	,,	8 34	9 41	12 46	2 11	3 37		8 5
Rhyl	,,	8 43	9 41	12 46	2 38	4 0		8 37
Chester	,,	9 20	10 20	1 30	3 25	4 48		9 52
Liverpool	,,	10 52	12 45	2 44	4 32	5 53		11 57
Manchester (Exchange)	,,	10 10	12 53	3 8	5 12	6 27		3 23
Birmingham	,,	12 17	12 41	4 18	6 41	7 24		2 33
London (Euston)	,,	1 40	2 10	5 40	8 10	8 50		3 50

					Sats only			
Blaenau Festiniog	dep.	7 45	7 45	9 35	12 20	2 45		7 5
Festiniog	,,	7 58	7 58	9 49	12 33	2 58		7 19
Bala	,,	8 48	8 48	10 44		3 50		8 11
Corwen	,,	9 24	9 24	11 46		4 43		8 45
Llangollen	,,	9 46	9 46	12 16		5 3		9 23
Chester	,,	10 35	10 35	1 13		6 0		10 30
Birkenhead	,,	11 11	11 11	1 45		6 45		11 10
Shrewsbury	,,	10 54	10 54	1 27		6 26		11*45
Manchester	,,	12 53	12 53	3 8		8 12		*Sats only.
Birmingham	,,	12 9	12 9	2 38		7 43		
London (Paddington)	,,	3 0	3 0	5 20		10 50		

A—Stops to take up or set down when required.

(Railway timetable, right-hand panel — G.W.R. / L.&N.W.R. / Cambrian Railways)

			p.m.	a.m.	a.m.	a.m.	p.m.
London (Paddington)	dep.	12*15				11 25	
Birmingham	,,	†Mon except 3*53				1 50	
Manchester	,,		7 40			1 5	
Shrewsbury	,,		6 30	8 0		2 35	
Birkenhead	,,		6 15	8 15		2 35	
Chester	,,		6 45	9 0		3 3	
Llangollen	,,		8 5	10 2		3 28	
Corwen	,,		8 21	10 29		4 22	
Bala	,,	7 35	9 30	11 34		5 35	
Festiniog	,,	8 27	10 23	12 35	4 50	6 30	
Blaenau Festiniog	arr.	8 43	10 40	12 40	5 5	6 45	

			Mid- n'g't		Sats only a.m.		
London (Euston)	dep.	10 0	12 0	5 0	8 30	10 37	
Birmingham	,,	11 0	2 50	7 20	9 55	12 15	
Manchester (London Rd)	,,	12 5		8 25	10 45	1 a 5	
Liverpool	,,	10 55		8 35	11 10	1 30	
Chester	,,	2 48	6 0	7 50	10 5	12 30	2 38
Rhyl	,,	3 35	7 12	9 5	10 50	1 14	3 16
Colwyn Bay	,,		7 43	9 35	11 13	1 35	3 33
Llandudno	,,		8 15	9 50	11 5	1 45	3 30
Llandudno Junction	,,	4 25	8 35	9 50	11 47	2 10	4 0
Bettws-y-coed	,,	5 25	9 14	11 0	12 27	2 52	5 2
Blaenau Festiniog	arr.	6 12	9 49	11 37	1 6	3 29	5 39

Down Trains.

			Ply 1	2	Sats only. 3	4	5	Sats exc'p 6	7
			a.m.	a.m.	a.m.	a.m.	a.m.	p.m.	p.m
Duffws	dep.	6 55	9 45	12 30	1 10	3 30	5 50	7 1
Blaenau Festiniog (G.W.)	,,				1 15			7 1
Blaenau Festiniog (L&NW)	,,	6 58	9 51	12 32	1 15	3 32	5 52	7 2
Tan-y-grisiau	,,	7 4	9 55	12 37	1 19	3 37	5 56	7 7
Dduallt	,,	A		12 45	A	A	A	A
Tan-y-Bwlch	,,	7 15	10 10	12 55	1 37	3 55	6 14	7 25
Penrhyn	,,	7 45	10 27	1 15	1 55	4 13	6 31	7 43
Minffordd	,,	7 50	10 31	1 20	2 0	4 20	6 35	7 50
Portmadoc (for Borthygest)	ar	8 0	10 40	1 30	2 10	4 30	6 45	8 0

Minffordd	dep.	10 35		3 37		6 40	8 40
Criccieth	arr.	10 55		3 55		7 0	8 55
Pwllheli	,,	11 20		4 20		7 25	9 20
Minffordd	dep.	11 15	2 7	2 7	4 50	6 48	
Harlech	,,	11 33	2 23	2 23	5 7	7 3	
Barmouth	,,	12 4	2 48	2 48	5 37	7 29	
Aberystwyth	,,	2 15	5 25	5 25	7 50	9 40	Sat only

A—Stops to take up or set down when required. *Exchange Station.

The opening of THE WELSH HIGHLAND RAILWAY has made it possible to travel between Dinas Junc. (3 miles from Carnarvon), South Snowdon, Beddgelert, the Pass of Aberglaslyn, and Portmadoc, where it connects with THE FESTINIOG "TOY" RAILWAY, which runs to Blaenau Festiniog. The latter railway, admired by people of many lands as a triumph of engineering skill, rises from sea level to a height of 700 feet, and throughout gives entrancing views of the Cardigan Bay Coast, the Snowdon Range, the beautiful Vale of Maentwrog, and the Mountains of Merioneth.

TIME TABLE (Weekdays only) from September 22nd, 1924 (Until Further Notice).

(Festiniog Railway and Welsh Highland Railway timetable, 1924)

		a.m.	a.m.	p.m.	p.m.	p.m.	p.m.	p.m.	p.m.
Blaenau Festiniog (G.W.R.)	dep.	9 18				3 40	4 25	6 40	
Blaenau Festiniog (L.M.S.R.)	dep.	9 20	12 28	12 57		3 42	4 29	6 43	
Tanygrisiau		9 27	12 35	1 4		3 49	4 35	6 50	
Dduallt						A	A	A	
Tanybwlch		9 48	12 57	1 26		4 11	4 57	7 12	
Penrhyndeudraeth		10 10	1 18	1 47		4 32	5 18	7 33	
Minffordd (for G.W.R.)	arr.	10 16	1 24	1 53		4 38	5 24	7 39	
Minffordd (for G.W.R.)	dep.	10 18	1 25	1 54		4 39	5 25	7 40	
Portmadoc (Old Station)	arr.	10 28	1 35	2 6		4 51	5 35	7 50	
Portmadoc (for G.W.R.)	dep.	9 10			3 45				
Pont Croesor		9A21			3A56				
Ynysfor		9A27			4A2				
Hafod Garregog		A			A				
Hafod-y-Llyn		A			A				
Nantmor		9A43			4A18				
Beddgelert	arr.	9 55			4 30				
Beddgelert	dep.	10 0			4 35				
Hafod Ruffydd		A			A				
Pitt's Head		A			A				
South Snowdon	arr.	10 10			5 5				
South Snowdon	dep.	10 45			5 17				
Quellyn Lake		10 58			5 30				
Salem		A			A				
Bettws Garmon		11 11			5 43				
Waenfawr		11 20			5 52				
Tryfan Junction		11 31			6 3				
Dinas Junc. (for L.M.S.R.)	arr.	11 40			6 12				

		a.m.	a.m.	a.m.	a.m.	a.m.	p.m.	p.m.
Dinas Junc. (for L.M.S.R.)	dep.	9 42				4 22		
Tryfan Junction		9 54				4 33		
Waenfawr		10 5				4 43		
Bettws Garmon		10 10				4 48		
Salem		A				A		
Plas-y-Nant		A				A		
Quellyn Lake		10 27				5 5		
South Snowdon	arr.	10 36				5 14		
South Snowdon	dep.	10 41				5 20		
Pitt's Head		A				A		
Hafod Ruffydd		A				A		
Beddgelert	arr.	11 6				5 45		
Beddgelert	dep.	11 10				5 50		
Nantmor		11A22				6A2		
Hafod-y-Llyn		A				A		
Hafod Garregog		A				A		
Ynysfor		11A38				6A18		
Pont Croesor		11A44				6A24		
Portmadoc (for G.W.R.)	arr.	11 55				6 35		
Portmadoc (Old Station)	dep.	5 15	5 45	6 15	7 50	11 5	2 20	5 10
Minffordd (for G.W.R.) arr.		5 25	5 55	6 25	8 0	11 15	2 30	5 20
Minffordd (for G.W.R.) dep.		5 26	5 56	6 26	8 2	11 22	2 31	5 27
Penrhyndeudraeth		5 32	6 3	6 32	8 8	11 29	2 37	5 34
Tanybwlch		5 57	6 27	6 57	8 33	11 53	A	A
Dduallt		A	A	A	A	A	A	A
Tanygrisiau		6 19	6 49	7 19	8 56	12 15	3 24	6 20
Blaenau Festiniog (L.M.S.R.)	arr.	6 25	6 55	7 25	9 2	12 21	3 50	6 26
Blaenau Festiniog (G.W.R.)	arr.	6 23	6 53	7 28	9 4	12 23	3 32	6 28

Notes:—A stops if required.

...engers to and from the Great Western Railway change at Portmadoc, Minffordd, or Blaenau Festiniog; and to and from the London, Midland & Scottish Railway ...inas Junc. or Blaenau Festiniog.

E. H. R. NICHOLLS, *Managing Director.*

FESTINIOG RAILWAY COMPANY

TIME TABLE

1957

WEEK DAYS, 5th JUNE—28th SEPTEMBER.
ALSO WHIT SUNDAY AND AUGUST SUNDAY

UP TRAINS

	A	A				B
Portmadoc	11.00	12.00	2.00	3.00	4.00	5.00	7.30
Minffordd	11.12	12.12	2.12	3.12	4.12	5.12	7.42
Penrhyndeudraeth	11.20	12.20	2.20	3.20	4.20	5.20	7.50
Tan-y-Bwlch							
Dduallt	Service temporarily suspended						
Tan-y-Grisiau							
Blaenau Ffestiniog							

DOWN TRAINS

	A	A				B
Blaenau Ffestiniog							
Tan-y-Grisiau	Service temporarily suspended						
Dduallt							
Tan-y-Bwlch							
Penrhyndeudraeth	11.30	12.30	2.30	3.30	4.30	5.30	8.00
Minffordd	11.38	12.38	2.38	3.38	4.38	5.38	8.08
Portmadoc	11.50	12.50	2.50	3.50	4.50	5.50	8.20

A. Week-days only, 15th July—7th September, also Whit Monday.

B. Tuesdays, Wednesdays, Thursdays, and Saturdays, 16th July—7th September.
Also Whit Saturday and Whit Monday.

All trains call at Pen Cob, Boston Lodge and Pen-y-Bryn halts by request.

All enquiries should be addressed to :—

The Manager, Festiniog Railway Company, Portmadoc, Caerns.
Tel. Portmadoc 2340   A. G. W. GARRAWAY, Manager

T. STEPHENSON & SONS LTD. PRINTERS, PRESCOT, LANCS.

TRAIN TIMES

PLEASE MATCH THE COLOUR SHOWN ON YOUR DATE OF TRAVEL WITH THE COLOUR CODED TIMETABLE BELOW

ALL TRAINS STEAM HAULED UNLESS OTHERWISE SHOWN

Every effort will be made to ensure running as timetable but the Ffestiniog Railway does not guarantee advertised connections nor the advertised traction in the event of breakdown or other disruption of service.

SAMPLE FARES

THIRD CLASS RETURN	ADULT	FAMILY (2 Adult and up to 2 children)
STEAM TRAINS		
Full Round Trip Portmadog to Blaenau Ffestiniog or vice versa.	£11.60	£23.20
Half-way Trip Tofft own Tan-y-Bwlch (National Park)	£7.80	£15.60

THIRD CLASS RETURN	ADULT	FAMILY (2 Adult and up to 2 children)
DIESEL TRAINS		
Full Round Trip Travel out by diesel Return by any train	£9.60	£19.20
Early Bird Travel to Blaenau Ffestiniog on the 0825. Return by any train	£7.60	£15.20
Tan-y-Bwlch Sorer Travel from Blaenau Ffestiniog to Tan-y-Bwlch on the 0940. Return by any train. Bargain Fare	£4.50	£9.00

THIRD CLASS RETURN	ADULT	FAMILY
SUMMER SHUTTLE		
Porthmadog to Minffordd	£2.50	£5.00

FIRST CLASS

Travel in luxury in the Observation Car or traditional vintage carriage compartments for an additional charge of £2.50 single or £5.00 return.

PLEASE ARRIVE AT THE STATION IN SUFFICIENT TIME TO CATCH YOUR TRAIN. BOOKING OFFICES CLOSE FIVE MINUTES BEFORE DEPARTURE TIME

Cash, cheques, Switch, Mastercard and Visa all welcome

Additional Fares Information overleaf

INDEX